D1270845

A
Temple
FOR
Tomorrows

poetry by

John Jeffire

AQUARIUS PRESS

Detroit, Michigan

A Temple for Tomorrows

© 2021 by John Jeffire

978-1-7357408-9-8

All rights reserved.

Cover photo: John Jeffire

LIVING DETROIT SERIES
AQUARIUS PRESS
Detroit, MI
www.AquariusPress.net

The author wishes to thank the editors of the following sources for publishing these poems: *the detroiter* ("Shoveling Snow In a Snowstorm"); *Midwestern Gothic* ("Birth Certificate"); *Paddlefish* ("The Horse and the Nail"); *In the Company of Writers Anthology* ("Hop In"); *Uncommon Core* ("Hesed"); *Life Preserved Anthology* ("An Abandoned Motel, Gratiot Avenue"); *Epigraph* ("Autumnal"); *The Gap Toothed Madness* ("Stray Cat" and "The Stray Dogs of Sochi"); *Right Hand Pointing* ("If That's the Best You Can Do"); *Lagan Online* ("The Place Where Poems Are Written"); *Dodging the Rain* ("A Bout of Heavy Drinking"); *Angry Old Man* ("Bump Stock," "Spondee," "Earthquake," "Bombing a Funeral," and "Bystander"); *Spank the Carp* ("Homage to Gene Rayburn, Daytime TV Gameshow Legend"); *Collateral* ("Seeing My Son Off to War"); *The Medical Literary Messenger* ("Emissary" and "Guest Lavatory, Beaumont Hospital, Day Five"); *The Five-Two* ("Ace"); *ImageOutWrite* ("Smear the Queer"); *Workers Write Journal* ("To My Student Being Deported"); *Strife and Harmony Anthology* ("Wonder Woman"); *Vita Brevis* ("Saudade II" and "Pre-Op"); *Backchannels* ("What's That Supposed to Mean?"); *Capable* ("Everybody Gets It But You," "Spoon Girl," "What We Talk About When We Talk About Love," "Saudade I," and "Love With a Dying Woman"); *The MacGuffin* ("Dogs and Ominous Weapons").

A number of these poems first appeared in the chapbook *Shoveling Snow in a Snowstorm*, which was published by the Finishing Line Press. "In a Time of Pandemic" will appear in *Capsule Magazine*.

The poet also offers deep thanks to Joy Gaines-Friedler, without whose patience, grace, and wisdom many of these poems would not appear or take the form they do.

Printed in the United States of America

Contents

I. Hustle

These poems are for my teacher—

Albert Glover—

"It's a strange courage…"

I.
Hustle

Birth Certificate

At exactly 6:25 a.m. on April 6th, 1962,
I sprung dumb from the viaduct gutter
Outside Detroit Mount Carmel Mercy Hospital
Backed up with rainbows of transmission fluid,
Sogged defeated leaves, frayed tire treads,
And a dead Doberman's decayed bald paw.
I was the 121st birth that day, one of 874,
All of us sharing Mickey Cochrane's birthday
Two months before he unstrapped his shinguards
And headed to the great dug-out in the sky.
E.W. Prichette, M.D., attendant at birth, confirms
I flushed full-formed from the East End's
Rectum, nickel pitching penis popping Hermes
With a stew-pot helmet, singing
The fight song of an ivy walled college
That would never accept me on
Its most deluded day. That morning I bit
My own umbilical and spit the shank
Of flesh tethering me to the assembly-
Line of blank bank statements of
An overdrafted confession booth
And cracked a tooth. On April 19th, 1962,
C.P. Anderson, M.D., officially registered
The birth on account I had not come to
My two-week old senses and cashed out
Of the madness early, instead opting to
Let life play out in its choking monotony,
Flunked science tests, cheating girlfriends,
Flat tires and empty gas tanks, a stay in the
County lock-up, bosses who cared less that
I was alive let alone born than the ex-wife
And my cable rep. All this was certified in 1988
By the Honorable Coleman A. Young, Mayor,
On behalf of the Detroit Department of Health.
So I now present this document, the official

Confirmation of my every failure to be someone
Other than a seven pound, 11 ounce ghost crying
And shitting his way into the world, demanding
Fifteen minutes of love and respect, a paper
Stamped by the Great Maker and Governor
George Romney and Mayor Jerome Cavanaugh
And anyone else who would listen that
Johanna Marie Kuzemka (maiden name),
Born in Donora, Pennsylvania, and her
Husband Thomas W. Jeffire, Jr., of Detroit,
An apprentice at the Ford Motor Company
Who was too stewed at Bookie's Tavern
On Washington Boulevard at Grand River
To realize he had a second son scribbled onto
His ledger of mouths to feed, had bestowed
A gift of some sort on humanity, ammonia
Breathed, shrieking at the Packard Plant off I-94
My birth and this day were truly like no other.

Bystander

july,   voice left
in the glove box with
the lighter—

it hits

freak   scream
glock pop
blur dumping
the burner on
picnic table
spread with   cold wings
and blue ribbons

you'd raise   a finger
if you could   move
cry out to

someone

thumb 911
hold   somebody
the little ones
get   under the table
just do   something
but everything's
on the backseat
windows rolled
dying   tongue
shot shut

Night, Engine, Brake Lights
—after Hayden

Hours after he suffocated the light
The light in our room and was sure
We were asleep, we heard the
Carkeys clink a jailbreak,
The deadbolt of the frontdoor
Clack open, steel-toed soles
On the porch, metallic click
Of car door, the emphysematic
Ford turn over in complicity.
When the red brake lights slapped
My brother's face, lit him
Demon wishing a four car pile-up,
I saw blood and brain on Michigan
Avenue, heard sirens and the coroner
Zipping shut his moloch eyes.

In the morning, television hanging,
Mother turned goblin with
Index finger to lip, eyes owl wide,
Each of us afraid to lift a toilet seat
Or close the cereal cupboard for
Fear of the cage locks bursting
Temple horn, spade tail, tusk.

Momma, just buy that gun.
Me and brother, we know
Where the hoods are hidden.
Fuse the inmate revolution.
Aluminum bat to tail lights.
Blow the driveway off the block.
Rat poison for the king rat.
Mr. Prick splayed on the power saw.
Take off. Go ahead, take off.
Take all the motherfucking off.

Coming Home, *Detroit*, 2015

He had your back at Packard
And the Rouge, told the story
You didn't even know you owned
On the bootlegger's pier off Atwater.
He walked Chevy in the Hole
In Flint as it gagged alkaline into
The undrinkable fecal river.
The girls at Café Chablis so tired
They didn't notice the gropers
Too tired to grope, but when
He heard Long Eddie on the
Alto he lifted a filmy boomba
And passed the salt at the Polish
Village Café over a steaming plate
Of stuffed cabbage and pierogis.
Hell, he's the one who chucked
The brick at the Overpass that
Clipped old Harry Bennett and
Left the prick in stitches before
He handed Frankensteen a hankie
To sop up the blood streaming
Off Reuther's mashed up face.
Behind the counter at Detroit
Transmission, he made damn sure
That all those briefcases of capped
Teeth and their bleached high-ball
Wives beside the club pool didn't
Dare equate you with the cairn of
Bolts and sheet metal humping the
Pointless cadence of your days.
 But you didn't know. How could you?
You can't name the last book you
Ever touched and can't claim to
Have ever finished one in your life.
And he was straight with that because

He understood how you returned
The punched time card to its smudged
Slot, found your hat and wool jacket,
Thermos and tin dinner pail, and
Headed to the monthly debt
On wheels where you pushed
The coffee-browned want ads
Off the front seat onto congealed
Food wrappers and empty waxed cups
With crippled straws still trying
                    To stand upright.
And he understood because he, too,
Had slid the key in the ignition
And turned, igniting no ideas,
No epiphanies, no way around or out.
He knew both what work was
And what it sure as hell wasn't.
It was his hand caught in the lathe,
His fingers on the shop floor.
The oil and grime beneath your
Remaining nails was his, and it would
Only flee if you peeled those nails
Back with plyers and sandblasted,
And for a split second you think
That might actually feel good.
The radio says someone important
Has died so you change the station,
Unwilling to feel any worse over one
More thing you can't change or undo.
You never met the man who rattled
The rag of your life on an upright
Wurlitzer missing half its keys, like
Rolling up the driveway to find
Some stranger has shoveled the
Walkway to the front steps where
Inside a woman awaits, brewing
You tea and fixing a ham sandwich,

The family dog near death at her heel.
And it's probably best that way.
You sit in the driveway a moment
For no reason, notice the way the
Moon defies darkness as daylight waits
Beyond the freeway to push them both
From the sky, flipping the headlights off,
Taking a good deep breath, performing
The daily sacred and silent ritual of
Sliding the transmission into park,
Reaching for the door latch, then
Stepping out into the burned air
To make your way inside.

—for P.L., 2/15/2015

Autumnal

stand of black ash, balsam poplar
arthritic elm
forest creeping silence
leaf echo orange to fire
green to sunlight
nostalgia plaqued on the brain
rustic dust wools the mantle

deer hovel, sleeping skunk
spine snapped
under car wheel
hand-laid footbridge
artemisian sludge

stone trail to sand
lake skin October caped quickens
salvo after gray salvo
whetted shale, pebbles
prehistoric detritus
immune as fish blood
each to the song
of its design

Earthquake

Maybe I ain't never been right but
sure as shit I been wronged, short
thug shunned an inch shy of the
coaster without his thickest soles.
Recognize the stare—dazed,
incredulous anyone's life could
be so full of electronic locks
and another shake down already
sounded before head count.
But it's not dazed—not really.
It's just the *why* of everything,
the can't-make-no-sense-of-it why
that refuses to slide like a chalked
cue in the augured groove
between thumb and index.
Your cellie stinks the stainless
commode, leaves pubes in the
sink, sprawls in the top tray
rereading letters he can't read,
ear buds plugged into the same
damn shit got him rolled up
in the first place. No sheets or
laces, fifty-two square of keep-yo-
ass-the-fuck-away, slipping
fungus toes into flip-flops
awaiting some good lookin' out
when the cement floor dances,
pod lights catch the DTs,
fingerprints flee the dayroom:
no use grabbin' onto nothing, man—
ain't no way out but out.

The Place Where Poems Are Written

It hasn't been swept or vacuumed in weeks.
Last night's shirt and socks drape the headboard,
A tabletop of pop cans and echoes from the attic.
We forgot whose turn it was to pay the electric so we
Sit dumb in front of open windows and commune
With unplugged fans, a week's groceries flatlining in the fridge.
The cell hasn't stopped vibrating a St. Vitus' bop
On the stained coffee table, but it's on its last charge.
We missed garbage day—raccoons scavenge the trash
For thigh bones and unlicked aluminum lids.

Amidst this—words.
Ribcage shelved with books,
Eyes repaned and caulked,
Lawn-watered mundane detritus
That defines us all—
Chaos, urge, the cleansing we must do.

Horse and the Nail

Every nail that lands a vein
It's my heart turns leather,
Unable to spit life into the next chamber.
The three-legged horse tripping inside you
Finds a girl at the bottom of the stairs.

You can stop falling.
The floor gets no less dirty.
   I surrender. Can you?

Nest

Second night on the recliner,
Broken shoulder slung,
The wife brings unsweetened tea
And Demerol, unfurls an
Extra blanket over my legs.
Earlier, she walked the dogs
With me when we came
Across a bird nest descending
From an electrical box suspended
On vinyl apartment building wall.
The dogs strained their leashes.
She found the featherless
Chick huddled in the dirt
With two cigarette butts, a
Splintered Bic, and a crushed
Plastic cap, blindly calling.
She handed her leash to my good arm,
The pulling dogs intent on the prize,
Retrieved the straining creature,
Returned it to the nest, which
She stuffed back up into the box.
We knew but hoped for the best,
Herded the dogs homeward.
In our closet, she finds
My winter hat on the floor
And pulls a featherless
Man from inside, penniless,
Supporting bones cracked,
Trust fled with the mortgage,
Lifts him slowly, tells him
What he's never heard before,
The twigs and twine and tatter
Of his days gathered and woven,
Sets him softly in his nest.

North Country

The mugs are never put away here,
And neither are their holders.
North Country winds heavy as
The truth you buried in your back
Too many years before, yet lump
To this hour. You know her name
But won't say it, not from pride,
Guilt, or regret, but just because it
Would do no good or change anything
Or ever agree to find its place.

Root

From the severed root
A hand reaches from the earth
Your eyes a sky of clear
Michigan October.
Even starlings quiet
Lone crows held on a rail fence
Along a rutted dirt road.
Fingers catch the morning new
In an orchard shorn
Of apples and peaches
Rise to the lake above.
The hurt root thickens—
No resurrection without death.
You are its blood instinct.
Its reason. Its hope.
What it must do despite
The hardening ground
Wet leaves sweet with decay
Worm, ant, raccoon scat
The yellowing life all around.
Reason is not carried on
The sharp drift of burnbarrel
Only your eyes, reason
Without reason, a sky of
Worn Michigan October.

An Abandoned Motel, Gratiot Avenue

No pack of guests pocketing wedding bands
Named Mr. Smith paying cash by the hour could
Have saved this empty place, and they didn't.
Checkered salesmen from Peoria journeyed
To worship so quickly the sheets never
Needed changing, just a spritz of Lysol,
And escaped before daylight in sedans
Whose trunks were stuffed with samples
So stupid they actually worked. The false
Eyelashes rinsed in the sink with a washcloth
Frayed at the edges, patted dry everything
That had turned sour in life, beginning
With the modeling job that required
A screen test in another room of this
Very building. The concrete blocks that
Formed this concrete block of manic lust
And loneliness have a couple stories:
One about a salesmen slipped on a slick
February sidewalk and the insurance
Unpaid in years, then over-ripe Cherry
Found three days decayed in a bathtub
Ringed in rust, strangled with her own
Stockings, her lipstick smudged, and
    No last name on the register.

A Bout of Heavy Drinking

I can't really say I lost track of time
So much as it lost all track of me.
I was always here, or maybe there,
Someplace, my bills mounting,
The exes hating me, my words
Circling in a holding pattern over
A pot-pocked parking lot, lights
Left on and battery stone dead,
Losing God and my car keys in
One fell swoop before happy hour.
So I took my stool, tossed a skin 20
On the bar, nodded to a bartender
Named Paulie and smiled at the barmaid
Who clocked in younger than my daughter
And cashed out with ten years on me,
looked up for a game, then settled in to weigh
The options one has when out of options.
I have no regrets save everything.
I have nothing to save save saving face.
Coasters replace. Shifts change. Mugs clink.
A few more 20s turn quarter and dime
And I am happy to not be unhappy.
I think of many things, see many
Faces, yearn for nothing more than
More time to sit, think, see, yearn.
I shift on my stool, empties elbowed
By buffalo tongue and pickled egg,
A splintered Indian and pretzel pieces
Left from St. Patty's day, an ice-filled steel
Trough to piss in that's always miles away.
I order words and the streets clear
Like a gunfight. No one knows me.
The earth will quake and flood, the sky
Disintegrate before my bloodshot eyes,
But I remain a head full of thoughts, in need

Of change and a few lies, lines, and
Lives that will form the tightest alibi
For who, what, and where I have been.

If That's the Best You Can Do

All breath begins in a desert,
Picking up sand and armies
And lifting them, scattering them
Where they will never be found.
Echoes replace what made them
And are replaced by cities, chrome,
And highways headed elsewhere.
This is where we choose: to be
Lifted from the earth and spat
Like a seed from the cannon mouth
Of a god, or to be lifted from
The earth and spat like a seed from
The cannon mouth of a god.

Ace

Johnny Ace step out his Caddy
Curbside the Page One, March
Evening, Detroit iced to the nostril,
His boy Lights Out undefeated
And Boom Boom on the get,
Johnny Ace rolling in green,
Yeah, you just wait, we just
Gettin' started, Holmes, this
Here ain't no nothin'.
That white flake shake three
Straight day, don't never slow—
I'm Johnny Ace, boy, you
Don't never call me Smith,
Not no chump hangin' off
The backside no red rig, naw,
Not no Gold Glove welter, naw,
Now we got diamond knuckles
Rollin' chrome spokes over 7 Mile.
Johnny Ace, he on the prowl, got him
Bennies to burn, Banks coyote coat,
Platform lace-ups, Boss Nigga lid
Like his man The Hammer, takin'
World the championship distance.

Then the roll up—
No make, no model, burners out.
This city, you pay up or you pay.
Blow gonna blow but the wind
Always forever rage in your face.
Bell don't even ring and Johnny Ace
Know the count, boom stick
And a 9 bark, five slugs dig
His ribs, lead kidney punch,
Jab jab to the chest, down
Go Johnny Ace, didn't nobody

See nothing, don't nobody know
Nothing when the coyote coat
Run red to the canvas, Johnny
Ace count the neons, point to
The stars, reach out for a rope
That wasn't never there.

—for Johnny Ace Smith,
murdered, Detroit, 37 years old,
10 March 1989

sonnit; i luv you suzi quatro-

the one true suzi q could ever do
first time i seen her i grew and i grew
i canned every can jus be suzi man
vinil undercuver creemy ham jam
jus one tuch suzi blak lether butt
lick this sick hunger from out my gut
fret my neck up to devil gate drive
teenage man handle throtled alive
detroit dinamo tenshin releiver
rolling stone cover plesure seaker diva
mi motor city missy thumpin her bass
trust mama gonna love sweet suzi face
  so we all come a stumblin to a 48 crash
  jus mash me back suzi slick licrish ass

2.23

Odometer measures
2.23 miles
the course is set
throw on sweatshirt
hoodie up
lace the shoes tight
I will run 2.23 miles

The ground is hard
the air carries nothing but
the same yellow-toothed virus
needing no airstream or
blue muzzle to the nape—
can't outjog it
can't skip around it
sure as hell won't
outlive it

It trails you
bores in on you
smokes you out and
drives you to a corner
daddy and junior
in the flatbed
gotta hunch, a suspicion
somethin' in the gut says
gonna justice somebody
got Roddie on vid'ya
paddy rollers unearthed
from ancestral long drop
dogs ain't needed
rising up in burned cross
goatee just an upsidedown
    hair hood
time was

                    time was
            sick nation gone
                          to sickness

            Today I run 2.23 miles

            The ground is hard
            pounding something back
            into me as I pound over it
            the sky broken into snow
            May still glinting
            February's armor
            the air carries nothing
            but the pig-necked garrote face
            world in the chest
            lead in the lungs
            and I run
            and I run

Homage to Gene Rayburn,
Daytime TV Gameshow Legend

In the mid-1970s when I became a teenager, my mother was in love with a TV gameshow host named Gene Rayburn. They met each weekday before dad got home, a little daytime tryst she never talked about but never missed. He could make her laugh—that was their secret. He wore crazy ties colored like sweet taffy and stuck his tongue out a lot, and when he smiled the TV screen filled with gleaming, oversized, too-white teeth crafted by an unimaginative Hollywood dentist of the time. I plowed through the front door after a tedious day chained in school and there she would be, folding the same clothes she folded yesterday, ashtray and coffee cup on the lamp table, and she laughed and laughed and laughed at this man named Gene Rayburn, who seemed to possess no special talents beyond reading his cue cards reasonably well and smiling with his oversized teeth and making overzealous contestants and not very famous celebrity guests and my mother laugh. And I laughed, too, not because Gene Rayburn was funny or anything he said impressed me one way or another, but because my mother laughed and seeing her laugh was a gift I could watch her open every day for the rest of my life.

Later, when dad's wheels took the driveway, the TV was turned off. The house conformed to programmed gloom. I found some homework to do. Someone who looked like my mother fled to the kitchen to check dinner.

Even at that age, I knew I would be a man like Gene Rayburn.

Dog

5:20 a.m. and I'm awake
to run exactly a mile
in Michigan darkness alone
outsmarting the judging
eyes of daylight
and my thin neighbors.
The sound of the frozen rubber
Of my tennis shoe soles
Is all that confirms my existence.
The headlights of a passing car
Beam me into a shadow trudging
The road's shoulder but soon
The clomping of my shoes
Again is all that exists.
Somewhere around the three quarter
Mile mark I spy an old woman
And an equally old dog.
My gait picks up.
The swelling of a reconstructed knee
And the bulging of weathered disks
Is nothing.

I can swear I am smiling.

Arthritic Roger Bannister
Is home in no time.

Of course,
We're talking dog years.

Explorer

When my bones were made of bone
I stood Penobscot straight
and made my declarations
to priest and beat cop with equal
parts kiss my ass and reverence.
I would scale garbage can and gutter
up to Mr. Neizio's garage roof
to pluck his dripping plums
or lift any rock to a Heaven
of my own choosing and creation.

I built my church and ripped it down
on a weekly basis, cornerstones
and rotary phones and zip codes
not one bastard's business but mine.
I detonated atom bombs in my
own backyard for the fuck of it
and smirked when I later learned
of something called radiation.
I told everyone I liked the heat.
What did I care? Whom did I owe?

And now. A stiff hip needs rest.
My own flesh and blood has
fled me like a tsunami village.
The women I pursue have children
with men I hope to never meet—
I am Christopher Columbus discovering
a land already trekked in footprints,
a people who already have names and a god,
bearing my seeping crotch of rot,
a hawk's bell, and a pouch of
jingly tinted glass beads.

Here, my beloved Taino, here is my open hand.

Fill it with your gold.
Your slim bones and bronze skin
I now claim for a queen who execrates me.
Bring me gold and your daughters and parrots
and I will build a flesh mound
of your severed hands.

Here, again, I hold out my hand—take it.
I will call you Indians.

Catechism

We sat as polished knobs,
our bobbing heads on springs,
performing our holy jobs
repeating sacred things.

When unruly eyes or wandering heads
strayed, Sister, armed with metal ruler,
rapped us from rapture until we bled
despite every covert ploy to fool her,

and yes, we wished her dead
with cancer and contaminated snot
despite all Jesus' words writ in red,
but a cuff on the head was all we got

and a workbook of lessons unlearned.
Yet we learned—to hate, to loathe—
which is exactly what we earned
years later, when we were all clothed

in divorce, jail, poverty, and shame.
Screw it. At least my knuckles healed.
Her words and threats were lame
as a jawboneless ass dead in a field

laid waste by grasshoppers and rot.
Hell, whether I want to admit it or not,
We deserved exactly what we got.

Smear the Queer
—for Kristine and Lea

Our smaller selves found no shortage
Of ways to shame the sensibilities of
The men some would one day become.
Listen and you still hear the cracking
Voice of puberty call out to the pack
Of mismatched socks and torn jackets
And kneeless jeans, behold the wave of
Churning legs bursting toward the far
Playground fence to safety, those in
The middle intent on corralling them
To the ground. Remember when old
Whitey drove Harvey to the dirt?
Run all he wanted, but wasn't nobody
Going to the Principal over that
Flat out creaming. And the time
Matty was rammed against the fence
And ganged by Rusty and Aaron?
Damn, smeared his nose all across
His girly face. And who didn't laugh
When Plato got drilled by Straight Hair
Willie and we high-fived to heaven?
At the teacher's whistle, we buried ourselves
In our smallnesses, years later to be outed
In public charades and masques of shame—
On those phobic fields of churned turf,
We learned to perpetrate the rabid little
Lynchings we as soon learned to forget,
Oblivious to those condemned and hunted
In blind boyhood's hangman complicity.

Peep Show

Two quarters bind a greasy pulp novel
Inebriated gyration typeset sentences
Grind house grammar and stiff red pen
Nylons scribbling down 42nd Street
Shimmy syntax the gardener invited inside
Butt crack sonnet oiled pube lube rhyme
Euro disco jazz an exclusive byline
Revised eyes glossed to confess
A polyester aftershave combover edition
Panting eraser palm in pocket
Dash of mustard mascara punctuated
On bloated silicone blurb mouth
Eternal inscribed 30-second love

Hesed

Before every leap
Appear several
Well-measured steps,
The kisses dreamed
Before the kiss.
So picture this:
A lifetime ago,
The crumpled old man
In the decaying frame
At the entrance
Is young and smooth;
As that young man,
He rolls his frayed sleeves
In the basement of
This very church
And shovels coal
Into a glowing furnace
Before winter sunrise
So the other worshippers
Have Sunday warmth.
Weeks turn years
And cross a century.
The coal dust
That settled into
The thumbs of his lungs
And squeezed the
Breath from him
And clung to his fingers
When he raised
The host to his lips
Meant nothing.
Yellowed photos
And fingernails and eye-whites
And a dying old man
Bleeding from his lungs

Are not this story,
But the black coal
Burning to whiteness
To warm those
Who would worship.

Stray Cat

Where there is a welcome
I am sure to wear it out—
The half gallon ice cream
Container sagging into
The sink, the family dog
Let out and forgotten,
Hope you weren't saving
That fifth of Black Label
For a special occasion, my
Those rib eyes were good,
Too bad you were at work,
Came across your car keys,
Didn't think I'd be gone so long.
It's a gift, really, to be invited
And then run on a rail, tried in
Absentia and hung in effigy from
The streetlight as warning
To neighbors, friends,
Relatives, and enemies alike,
Skinned and fileted into
Dumpster rat sushi and
Skull fixed on a pole.
But we stray cats have more
Than nine lives—we snoop
Extras from under the door mat,
Taped to the bottom of the
Sock drawer, wedged between
The leaves of moldy books,
Barter a few spares with bookie,
Loan shark, and pawn broker.
We are born to practice the
Ultimate Cheshire defiance,
Looking off to the litter box
Gleaming beside the Frigidaire
As we flood the heirloom rug

For the Anniversary of My Death

—after Merwin

My friend Khuzin from Russia
Messages me happy birthday.
In Russia, it is already Thursday,
But for another hour or so
I am still in Wednesday and
Can claim to be a year younger
Than he knows me to be.
Somewhere in the great unlived,
A silence will sound where
The last fires bow then lay still,
And a friend in some distant timezone
Will mention my passing while
My lips touch glass one last time,
Content, not yet privy to the news.

What's That Supposed to Mean

I don't suppose it's supposed
to mean anything.
Humpback carcass washed ashore
supposes nothing but chainsaws and pick-ups,
ruined gloves and blood-sogged boots left outside,
the beach needing a good hard rain.
It means dead.
It means these things happen:
Dog lapping mortal wound,
life's waning instinct,
the affirmation of blood.
At the end of the end,
I suppose it means that as
I grow older my poems
      grow shorter,
aphasia's blessed plague,
nothing I need to say
that can't be said simply,
incoherently, incompletely,
the lint catcher raked,
pentimento bleeding,
powered off mid-thought,
package with no return address
abandoned on the stoop.

A Middling Talent of Negligible Import

Cans not fans or canons await.
Not even fat enemies at your gate.
No remembrance, no footnotes,
no references, sorry, no flash.
Fries will never come with that,
cheese extra if we had it, outgoing
flights cancelled, no rescheduling,
all sales final, no returns.
The words can always
be recycled, donated to those
less unfortunate, someone
who could actually use them,
style too banal, too mild to elicit
enough bile for even a bad review.
Kindling, cat box liner,
book marks for real books,
not one snide or funny look,
me dumpster, me hungry.
Salieri's dumb brother, no Dryden
to your Flecknoe, the Pope
shorn bald of locks, unearning
a lusty excommunication,
reinstatement without a state,
the grand buffet without a plate,
unable to demand removal
from a call list you never made,
the Revolution will not be scheduled
let alone televised.
And no, don't call back later,
don't leave a message because
there is no beep,
we don't encourage you
to keep us in mind for
future submissions,
at no point in this lifetime

will we look forward to
reading more of your work.
      You, fool, wake up:
Do yourself a favor, pull the plug.
Hide that nasty sty under the rug.
Create an alias, hit the jug.
Neither bone nor catalog
for you, neutered dog,
kissed prince forever a frog.
Boy, you in the wrong hood for love—
So dig, man, dig 'til you're dug.

Shoveling Snow in a Snowstorm

Bulimic Michigan winter belches
Gusting bowels of whiteout fury,
Green Ford pick-up engulfed
Beneath blind waves of ice,
Neighbors' homes capsized
In a squalling January tempest.
Wife marooned at work,
Kids swept away to college,
I abandon ship through the front
Door portal, wind tidalwaving
Into the foyer, intruder shouldering
Into the house, until I find myself
Cast adrift in the driveway
Clinging to a rusted shovel.
Cheekskin freeze-dried in air,
Fingertips vaporized in thermal glove—
There is absolutely no point
To what I am about to do.
It'll make it easier when the snow
Finally does stop someone who looks like me
Says inside my brain, the stupidest idea I've
Tried to convince myself of in months.
A snowmobile sails by in the street
And a mitten waves joyously.
I've shoveled snow my whole life
And where has it gotten me?
More snow always falls.
Shovels break, back muscles give,
Seas of breath lost in a flurry of grief.
I awaken to the sound of aluminum
Scraping along frozen cement.
The sky is an ocean of whirling stars.
It's snowing out. And me? I shovel snow.

II.

What Rough Beast, Its Hour Come Round

Bombing a Funeral

Sheathed cyanide seed
Palled aloft,
Throng wailing—
     Eardrum burst.
Knee surge,
Body throttled,
Mind blown,
Skin stripped,
Bone shredded,
Rocket flak
Car hull turned
Grenade, tattered
Ball bearing
Vest of Satan—
Black suits
Black dresses
Black hats
Burned black
Blown bowels
Blood sod.
Pine box
Blasted
Brain matter
Flecked in beard
No matter
But the funerals
Of those who
Walked this one,
Their funerals
Breed funerals,
The dead burying
The dead burying
The dead in Sanaa,
Hay Al-Amal,
Abadam Faransa,

Suruc and Zamalka
One funeral becomes
A dozen becomes
A thousand as the
Eyeless dead hum
The harvest dirge.

Seeing My Son Off to War

You're no writer, he tells me
the night before, well-rationed
with tequila and draft beer and
sandbox testosterone, and I say
nothing because I am as drunk
as he is and I don't want to argue
and I have no counter-attack
even if I did. This morning, his
last leave before deployment ends.
I doublepark in the dark outside
domestic departures, he pulls
his bag from the back seat,
a walled city between us.
Eyes meet and cover, dumb
hands pinned in pockets until
there is nothing left to see or
say or pretend we must say.
We shake hands. When I slap
his shoulder in male ritual,
I hear the nut-quake detonation,

see the lens of a correspondent's
camera flecked with blood,
smell the rubberized vinyl
guaranteed not to leak.
I want to warn young Telemachus
of Circe's bed, reveal the trick
to stringing the heirloom bow,
tell him to keep heads up for
a one-eyed, blind giant prick with
a bone to pick staggering the Tigris,
but last night Athena misplaced the moon
the more we reloaded our cups,
the bow snapped like a winter twig
and tossed at the feet of some fool
　　　sewing his fields with salt.

The time for words is dismissed.
At the curb, he nods, we regroup, he
turns his back one last time to face
wars, wars, wars—those fought,
those to be waged, father and son
mapping the prophesied waters.

The Diplomat

Cracked slate roofs, pitted street,
Gargoyles and saints on strike in
A discarded century—
Nude, he surveys the breadth
Of this adopted city from
The balcony of his rooms.
His nose wrinkles above
A mustachioed lip, the
Cancer burn of factories
That line the mucous river.
Cummerbund and ballroom replaced
By ashtray, cellphone, and appointment.
A mint leaf in a pinky tea cup.
Goulash simmering on a gas stove.
A corkscrew and a bottle of local.
If the townsmen knew you called him,
Craved the kindling of his touch,
They'd chase you pitchforks and
Torches to an abandoned windmill.

Not one dog howls the misted moon.
No drunks fight over crusts and dregs.
Alone, his continent a galaxy away—
Even the natives desert this place.

To My Student Being Deported

My training conditions me to not judge
Your total lack of observable interest
In my class or anything I say—sometimes
Miracles emerge with love and patience.
Each time I asked when you would turn in
Your missing work so you could pass,
You politely lied that it would all be in
At the start of next week, and of course
I was wise to never hold my breath
For every next week that passed.
Your name pegged you to the bad
Side of the Adriatic, flesh trafficking
In the streets of Tirana transformed
Into a Coney Island restaurant on Gratiot
Or a party store front off Chalmers.
I said I stayed away from judgment,
But after class one day you approached
Me in the hall pleading a favor.
Not the extension on late work I'd hoped
For or a chance to negotiate a D-, nothing
So meaningless as that. No, it seems
That Uncle Sam had caught up with
All your changed addresses, the weeks
In an uncle's basement, two months
In the storage room above the used
Car dealership, hitting this dead end:
The summons your mother received
Never reached her in time to put
On an Americanized face in court
And plead her child's case.
        So it's come to this.
The fact that you are coming to me
Speaks your desperation, a teacher
From whom you've earned straight Fs.
You politely ask me if I would please

Compose a letter that will in some way
Convince the judge who issued
Your deportation orders that
You are indeed a human being,
One who breathes, one who can
Prove his allegiance to the flag
And our cultural values by reciting
The lyrics to five Kendrick Lamar songs,
By rushing the drive-thru at least
Once a day at McDonald's,
By sporting Kenzo jeans
And the latest Affliction T's.
But I need more than your outside
Yankee-ized smile and gelled hair.
How have you done in other classes?
 Like yours.
Do you play any sports, represent
The school in any way?
 No, no social security number—
 If I get hurt, I can't see a doctor.
Well, what about a job, helping
Support your family, looking after
Younger brothers and sisters,
Anything I say to the judge to convince
Him you will be a productive, contributing
Member of society if pardoned?
 I'm the youngest. No official job.
 My father works 60 hours
 A week at a relative's, all under
 The table, so we can't say
 Anything about work.
 I fix cars for my friends.
 I'm a good mechanic.
I assess the situation and my
My potential quarry, a judge
With not one donor dime
On the line or vote in the pot,

55

A lunatic constituency drunk
On xenophobic hate.
Xhavit, I will only admit to you
Now that I lied gently for you—
Yes, I told the truth when I
Said you were a polite, respectful,
Kind-hearted young man.
I can stand by all that.
But I mentioned nothing of your grades
Or total lack of effort in my class, saying
Only that you have lived a very stressful life,
Moving often, no chance to make
Longterm friends, no driver's license,
No sense of place—fearful.
That was the poet in me, using a little
License to fill in the gaps strewn
About your pot-holed history.
I said you hoped to become a mechanical
Engineer and not just a plain mechanic,
But that's on me, not you.
I lied because I saw you willing to become
No more or less than what your American
Peers will become, another face in
Our national team picture, someone
Who will feed the quotidian need,
For a plasma screen TV, more mouths to feed
With Monsanto seeds and a dream
Tucked securely in a billfold filled with
With paper and plastic.

On Monday after class, I quietly hand you
An envelope with my letter.
You smile, thank me, shake my hand.
On Tuesday, you have dropped out of school.
I take roll and begin my lessons for the day.

The Nickel of Truth
"We hold these truths to be self-evident..."

It doesn't buy much anymore,
But if you save enough of them
You can pay to replace the knees,
Aortic valves, disks, and dreams
You obliterated in their saving.
On one side, you've got shiny
Tom Jefferson looking off to Sally
Hemings' quarters, hawking
Liberty and trust in god like
A plaid car salesman. On the
Flip side we covet Monticello,
Where he and Sally's mulatto
Children earned no last name,
No declarations or inheritance,
Just the right to be purchased in
Louisiana and a daddy too busy
Forging paper freedoms to
Come say hello in the fields.

The Last Jew of Vinnitsa

Victory is hard work but Bingel
Says we are nearly finished
And we are all eager to be home.
I carried bag after bag of lime
To the edge of the pits
And it was greatly tiring.
With such victory, the war
Will be over very soon.
We are all ready for holiday.
It was rather funny that we told them
They were to report for a census
Near the airfield and then had them
Place their valuables on the tables.
Can you imagine their surprise?
It was great sporting fun.
I have secured a rather nice ring
And a few other such items for you.
I hope that you are pleased.
The airplane engines are very loud
And hurt my ears severely.
I have been eating well enough.
The sausage here is passable
        But it's not home.
The temperature is agreeable
And the locals are friendly enough.
Some of the natives have even
Been enlisted to assist in the process.
Vinnitsa and nearby Uman
Are pleasant enough
        But it's not home.
These people truly disgust me
And I am glad to be rid of such filth.
They took off all their clothes, even
The women, and showed no shame.
Toward the end we did not even

Bother to have them undress
And just finished our job as is.
I am most proud to be a member of
Einsatzgruppe D and the work we do.
They are a fine group of fellows
And most fun to share a beer with.
Can you believe the final count
Topped the 28,000 marker?
The leadership is very pleased with us.
Victory, though, is very hard work.
I am anxious to walk with you
Along the river and hear the sweet
Music of your voice.
The Umanka is a stream of swine piss
Compared to the Rhine.
The work is finally done.
Victory is hard work but
Bingel says we are nearly finished.
I have a tooth that is rotting
And smells most horrible but I shall
Have it fixed before I am to you.
I've enclosed this picture
To show you what we do.
The nerve of that shitty fellow.
Regards to all loved ones at home.
To think, it is almost October.

It's One Thing to Die on a Pile of Brass

I.
Rule one:
Never pull a trigger unless
It's to kill.

II.
Bad ju-ju.
Training mission after range time
But secondary weapon, sidearm,
Never cleared.
Kid playing enemy forces.
Private, nineteen, from
Bumfuck, US of A.
First, never cleared.
Second, safety off.
Third, you never fucking pull
That trigger unless it's to kill.

III.
Plugged armpit to armpit.
Lung, heart, spinal column, lung.
Everything needed to live
Shredded. Chin specked
In blood and pimples.
Official letter home:
It is our sad duty to inform you...

IV.
No life expectancy here.
The hadjis drive batshit.
A pick-up with at least
A dozen in the bed

Weaving two wheels
In and out of the convoy.
Setting the ambush?
Creating the distraction
That leaves a Humvee
An oven of body parts?
Take them out with the 50?
No, just asshole kids who
Know they won't live long.
They don't care.
No reason to.
Lock on, just in case,
But let 'em go.

V.
We are ordered to a meal
With their officers.
Everybody here is a general.
Or a colonel. Fuck that.
Their hands are everywhere,
In everything.
We address each other as
General Solo, Field Marshall Diddy,
Colonel Kardashian.
We understand nothing
They say, don't really care to.
They eat everything,
Flashing tobacco teeth.
Our smiles are field manual.
One, two days after the last
Of us is allowed to leave,
These generals and colonels
Will all swing above the Tigris.

VI.
You learn things here.
Human bone melts at
3000 degrees Fahrenheit.
Vulture clips a power line
And nosedives two kilometers
From the FOB.
Two pogues ejected on impact.
Five crispies inside melted
Forever to their bird.
We watch for six hours,
Ravens on a power line.
The smell, the CO says,
You'll never forget it.
Jet fuel and flesh head,
Hands, and feet, offerings
No decent god would touch.
You learn things here.
You learn things.

VII.
No rules here.
They drive the wrong way
Down a divided highway
T-boned by their brothers.
The local police sweep
The litter, human stew,
The road reopens stained red.
Christ, take me in a firefight,
Merc us all in an ambush,
Trigger fingers amped,
Eyes open until the end.
How many times have we
Talked about this. Every

Fucking time, we talk about it.
We'll go down on a hot pile
Of brass casings but, man,
Just not like that kid.
No, not like that kid.

Spondee

Who me?
Yeah you.
What's next?
You're up.
Hold up.
Sit down.
Stand up.
Shut up.
Go back.
Wait here.
Buy now.
Fuck yeah.
Fuck no.
Fuck you.
Fuck me?
Fuck off.
Fuck all.
Fuck head.
Fuck it.
Eat shit.
Eat out.
Eat here.
Eat me.
Live well.
Lights out.
Some friend.
Makes sense.
Live long.
Love strong.
Laugh deep.
Be free.
On guard.
Click bait.
Fake news.
Hear me.

Get up.
Get out.
Get off.
Get down.
Bed time.
Be kind.
Pay up.
Step up.
Screw up.
Dumb shit.
Let's dance.
Not now.
No hope.
Not once.
No way.
Fat chance.
Bite me.
Fat free.
Love you.
Call me.
Write soon.

Bump Stock

And so again to gather ye
Upon the hallowed floor
32 stories above which
The sacred fell the sacred floor
Those noble 59 did not
Sacrifice their rights so that
You could seize mine
With ear upon freedom's door
As forefathers conceived this
Day forth a new militia
Quothing ever or nevermore
Dedicated to the inalienable
Well-trained eye to stand
Its ground and pound into
Submission all ye who threaten
The fruitful grain we stored
By the truth in the night nor
Human hand nor eye dare
The gore we bore this shore
Hireling or slave to this very
Flag we kneel in anthemic
Amendment thusly four score
I can tell you this believe me
Let taps ring and sing as forth
Bags and caskets we smiling bring
To bump the association stock
For whom the closing bell tolls
Hand over heart…and mouth
And eyes into star-spangled house
Divided our heroic lead pours
These simple oaths we swore
More blood, more barrel, more

The Stray Dogs of Sochi

This one scratches the fleas he picked up
In the cliffs surrounding Kabul. He answers
To the name Sasha, or Pasha, or Vladi
And he clearly remembers the fresh purple
Lotus bulbs burst from the fields pure
As that first hit from a comrade's pipe.
When the clouds of happiness no longer
Lifted the Taliban dagger dancing
Across his throat, he loaded the glass Scud
And sailed cosmonaut over the Volga.

Wandered west from the same bastard litter,
Keisha holds a markered cardboard collar
That reads, "Please feed my child."
Grenade haired, one unfocused eye
Hocking puss, her arms are tracked
From the foot of Mayor Cobo's Arena
To Herman Gardens, to a trap house
Two blocks off the Edsel Ford Freeway,
To an abandoned factory guarding
The Motor City Casino, to the slumping
William Livingston house at Brush Park,
Albert Kahn's purebred puppy hacking dust.
Here at a corner before Madison Avenue
Jogs onto 375, this stray begs bones
As a roach burrows into the darkness of
A cot at the Wayne County lock-up,
Hey, y'all hold that shit down, Lebron
James is explaining destiny on ESPN.

The Ritual

I have too much to do
And too much time to do it,
And so nothing gets done.
Desperation humming blood
Like an archaic gas house
Furnace belched to life.
Now, act of self-discovered
History, carving elaborate
Designs on my cheeks and
Forehead with a razor.
Curly-cuing great birds and
Half human cats that dance
The countenance of my tribe.
I will wipe away the blood
And let the scars scab down.
Healed, I will enter a new
Sunlight and tell the trees,
Pointing to the ridged scar
Letters of a fantastical world,
Here, I am arrived.

The Liver Is the Cock's Comb

Swinging prick swagger, filter of toxins
In mad reverse flooding the heart's mind
With shapes and landscapes and visions
Of the nymph's exposed ribs and Ararat
Brushed from the dripping globe,
The cock of the walk preening then
Combed over double in a gutter the next,
A red wheelbarrow full of banana pratfalls
Where the joke was always on him.
Crush the cockhat beneath severed heel,
Whether you're too chicken or not
Not chicken enough, once the fool's cap
Is donned the self-con is on—days from
The spine's break, a wife spent of
Spending time tending atrophic hand,
Barnfire ignites vanity that is the unlived
Liver's curse, gold and fire spikes drinking
Sinking wreckage on the black swamp
Laughing in the liver's last bitter bile.

George Antal (1922-1943)

A Navy machinist's mate second class, he died on November 24, 1943, when his ship the USS Liscome Bay was torpedoed by a Japanese submarine. He was 22.

o   ce

an

C   A

ocean

e

ce   an

o

N

ocean

o   c

ean

ocean

ocean

o

c

e

a

n

remembered

70

Dogs and Ominous Weapons

you wanna shut me up
you gotta bust my mouth
or break my will—
one don't think you can do
other i know you can't

two pandemics
smog my oxygen
both at my throat
both cinch the windpipe
clog the lung
both look at me
with blue animal eye

dogs ain't new boss
400 years of dogs
and i'm still here
no more places to run
all weapons ominous
rubber bullet
        still a bullet
mean the same thing—
one kill me straight out
other kill me over time
torch the fuse that light
a thousand fuses
both glove your throat
same knee to neck conclusion
human life turned hashtag
maybe one day
even kill *you*

George Perry Floyd Had C-19

Two pandemics loosed
on his skin.
Two viruses loosed
in the streets.

One, he had a chance.

Sine Nomine

A man with a name commands
a thousand without
to turn his fields
in their still-warm blood,
stack his wall with
each other's skulls,
glisten his boot
with their parent's
marrow. In exchange
the man with a name
hands over a map
to his grain stores
with a harlequin voucher
past its redemption date—
believe me, one must be
smart to earn a name,
one that will be paid
into history books,
memorized by the children
of those without one,
open mouths fed
words and letters
that will never spell or
utter anything for them,

first, last, or middle.

The Welterweight

—for Luke Marcelli

One fight is the last.
He stands, head bowed
beneath arena torches,
blood merum coursing
from his brow,
awaiting decision—
a scale always tipping.
So he trained, beast to
the hours of bone
leveraged against bone,
the fibers of muscle
torqued to newer limit,
the stone cries of trainer
banishing the mind's whisper
to turn back from someplace
never seen, never touched,
never believed but dreamed.
In the end, one hand is raised,
a boy falls from the sky as
the lights dim, a new rain
washes the red arena floor
of both victory and defeat,
the backs of the spectators
fill the eastern gate as you
trek to the west, timeless,
throbbing, clean, spent,
memory of the beating heart
called to some other purpose.

The Movable Ladder

Remember this:
Where Helena stepped
Venus fell, the earth bubbling
Crosses—her son who hung
His own son and boiled
His wife alive, unholiest
Of broken holy lineage.

Remember the edifice itself
Razed and restored, rebuilt
And raised as the One for
Whom it was built on the
Ground of His rising.

Remember, a ladder is meant
To climb, to rise above,
Six rungs for six hands,
For Greek to raise Armenian,
Coptic to reach to Syrian,
Roman to Ethiopian.

Remember, each hand no
Matter its color or the book
It holds, whose hair it strokes,
Shares the same count of fingers,
Mottles the same with age,
Bleeds with every blow
It delivers and fends.

Remember, rise up, people,
Reach to one another,
Rise, climb together, *rise*.

How We Heal

We claim the year the locust has stolen
With hearts made soft by the mallet rain

Of bad fate and the hard acrid fire
Of its blackened face. Think of an inferno

Filtered through a glass of wine—
Humility drills the skin of our self

To the self within, the ghost inside
The apparition. How we change we

Cannot say but that does not stop our tongue.
We're poured the mute cup of suffering

Because we can stomach it and pledge
Obedience to pierced palms and riven side.

And the truth? We are the cup from which we drink,
The bent stem, split lip, and battered body:

We mend in the presence of those more broken—
Extending a fractured hand to fill the cup again.

We Carry the Dead

"Her tour of grief is now over..."
—The Center for Whale Research

Seventeen days over one
Thousand miles, Salish water
A white froth of finned horses—
Tém, q'ell·álĕmĕčĕn, sqḭḷĕlĕs.
The dead a body we push ahead,
Drag behind, nose to the surface,
A father's quick fist, mother's
Small open hands, the mate's
Bed-warmth pulsing jug
Of summer moonlight—
Buried deep in the folds
Of gut and bone until let go,
The natural weight pulling
At all we know, the dead
Releasing the dying who
Cling to what they soon
Can no longer hold.

In a Time of Pandemic

I.

Garbageman strides Apollo,
Young woman stocking
Grocery shelf floats.
Streets deserted of their
Spiced echoes, wind stripped
Of the scent of faces.
I help the neighbor woman
Corral her dog as she carries
Her shopping inside.
The man across the street
Has added more guns—
Long rifle and sidearm,
When it comes down to it,
The survivalist's full assault
Into your food supply.

My house is empty of all
But myself, my wife, two
Perked dogs awaiting a walk,
The remaining wine and toilet paper.
If I go out hungry, my friends,
I go out full

II.

The window, gray landscape.
I am my wife after five brain surgeries,
Limp, trapped in a car pushed
Off the pier, soup spooned
To gasping mouth.
I am a fall of black mane
Writing a candlelight diary
In a frozen attic.
I am five inch-thick bars and
A green stool on Robben Island,
Mind and hands and manacles
Whetted by limestone.
I am wanderer in a 6 x 9 desert,
Four walls the corners of Judea,
Not one temptation to resist.

Bird.
Barren branch teased by wind.
Sudden passing car lightless
Gloved mask at the wheel

III.

The first retreat, inside,
Hearth, water, rice, black tea,
One retreat tailed by another,
Under roof then dig inward,
Mine into dark pith.
Inside, what we stored,
Stacked, froze, buried,
What we locked away
Mostly from ourselves,
Saved for something, someone,
Touching a bare wire, eyes
Burned with acidulant day,
Rummaging the wreckage,
No letter or confession,
Just the dress bought for her
That she never wore, or wore
Smiling for someone else
In some other chamber

IV.

You will flatten curves
for the rest of your days,
and your children, and
                    theirs.
And they won't flatten
because that's the thing
about a curve, how it
refuses to straighten up
no matter how many times
you slap its punk face,
like how not even a hoax
is ever really a hoax if
you must pause before
affirming your own lips,
to feel them as some
stranger's fingers,
stop dead and gather
your purse at every
shadow and footstep,
a loon with a screwdriver
to your temple,
every cough a spittle
of death bursting
a Dachau air duct.
And say there are hoaxes—
you can't fully contain them,
and there will never
be a reliable test
or enough of them
even if there were.

These are facts:
boxed bodies line
a trench on Hart Island
and the zippered slump
in recliners in Detroit,
stack themselves like
garment bags in the morgue.
Nothing magically disappears
with Spring.
Touch your face.
Breathe your lover in.
It's okay—
all ends cloaked in
distance we never
sought to maintain

III.

Tomorrows

Found

We met when we met—
A day sooner or later and
This key would not turn no
Matter how hard I jiggled it.
You, winter cloaked
And scarved aglow,
Your grin out-watting
The pinball machine in
The neutral ground of
A local pub, plenty of
Witnesses—blind date
Blindside sideshow shot.
       So I took it.
We embraced, I felt
The brittleness of your
Spine and ribs beneath
The calliope piping of
Your hummingbird song.
If you whiffed gin on my
Breath you never cashed in as
I crashed glad-giddy deep
In your charm. That night,
Shins and elbows enmeshed,
we crooned a flesh duet
Our own until jelly toast, coffee,
And eggs became plane tickets,
Luggage, a lease, and a plate of God's
Promise heaped high with peace.
Woman, I've covered gray seas
And ground my rickety knees
To the caps to heal a torn hemisphere,
   And in this finding I am found.

Dare Devil

You hadn't been christened yet
But I somehow called out to you
By name, waving amidst your minions
As you deplaned, windsheared
Off the morning Midtown bus.
The flutter of those hummingbird
Lashes melted me like a tongue-dying
Popsicle you can't lick fast enough
Dropped on a runaway July runway.
I swigged the chocolate in your eyes
In one of those I-don't-know-you-
But-I've-known-you-my-whole-life
Auto-pilot moments, and you pulled
Me aboard your barnstorming
Wing to flap the Charleston
blindfolded, but I didn't bail.
We barrel-rolled a barrel-house of
Top-shelf cackles and bar-well nuts—
Mile high, cockpit secured, I banked in.
Now, the devil may care but when
He's due then to hell with the chutes,
The black box and alerting the tower,
Prepare for take-off, this flight
Has no set destination but a galley
Full of grins, oceans in the overhead bins,
Bombs away and into our wild yonder.

Hop In

No argument, we're all total carwrecks,
Samsonite blown off the trunk,
Soiled underwear and dryer burned shirts
Tumbling over the highway, loonies freed
From the asylum. Whose job it was
To tie the baggage down now moot
As the coffee stained map ten years
Out of date, charting a course on a stretch
Of two-lane road turned stripmall.
But there you are, lady, thumb up,
Cherry licorice stick legs and high beam
Smile hoping one more ride, safe passage
On a well-lit, smoothly paved freeway
To a gated community still on its hinges.
I'm not hiding my dented fenders,
Defective doorlocks and cracked windshield.
Coincidence, but I'm headed wherever
You're going, so hop in, buckle up, find
A favorite station on the radio, there's still
Gas in this tank and tread enough to burn.

Kintsukuroi
—for Konnie

She sets sail by stars to a wreck of reef
Submerged in shadow. Adrift, a stormleaf
That cannot settle, this woman I've braced
Tremoring as she relives the quick taste

Of her own blood spotting a kitchen floor.
I stand watch on shore. I release the door,
Hold of pain, sirens singing memory
Through the keel, whispering that all will be

Whole, swept away, the calm he shattered quick
As her wrist pieced, battened, the fog wall thick
But a course waiting to be mapped. I hear
My own words and taste the salt in her fear.

Gold and God find the fissures, flood the breach—
This mended vessel weathers every sea.

The Ides of Everything

Most times you don't know until after it's
Over and you limp back, divide by two, and
There you were, mid-sentence, a rare coherent

Thought, a drowning relationship, a raging war
Everyone knew would never go the distance.
Perhaps somewhere in that middle you longed

For the beginning, ached for an end, or relished
The undefinable betweenness of the moment.
Yet the math we are taught is so often untrue.

You see, there are some people, like my wife,
Beautiful even when they sleep, so much so
She has no beginning, no middle, no end.

After she wakes, after I've looked everywhere,
In the glovebox, under the sofa cushions,
The basement behind the hot water heater,

I still find no middle, no beginning, no end.
I look but only see her constellation eyes, wander
Her rainforest legs, grateful to rest at a place
I hope is somewhere in the middle of things.

A While

Is it more than a moment or less than a time?
No one knows, and what part of it is yours and

what part mine no one can say for sure. So
our shoes rest at the door, our coats on the sofa's

back. The dogs perk at our feet, tuned to our
every motion, our every letting go of breath.

I can only stay a while, and you the same.
We absorb all light through the sitting room

windows until the sun must leave us. Soon
the stars will let loose their hair and shimmer.

A little while longer—bread bestowed and received,
Shared in the long shadow of our shadow.

Emissary

An old man pushing an even older woman
In a wheelchair. Assumption, mother and son.
His mustache tobacco stained, and somehow
One wheel has locked, so when he tries to push her
Into the awaiting hospital elevator, she spins a circle.
I've been here, what, five, six, how many times
Since last winter gave up its blades waiting for someone
To explain the why behind my wife's suffering.
And so? I am polite, foreign emissary without
Credential, stamped dispatches, an official seal.
I step into the mouth, hold it at bay: when he frees
The wheel, I motion him and the woman inside.

Guest Lavatory, Beaumont Hospital,
Day Five

It has a place to urinate.
A place to brush my teeth.
Space enough to throw
a sleeping bag or
some newspaper.
A paper towel dispenser
and plenty of toilet paper
and fresh-smelling soap.
A strong lock and
bright lights and two
outlets to charge the cell
and a table to change a baby
or to set a laptop
with free wi-fi access
or to eat a styrofoam plate
of cafeteria spaghetti
or to kneel before
and beg miracles,
a mirror to confirm
what's left of my face.

I, guest, squatter, husband,
survivor of my wife's survival.
Really, I could live here.

Saudade I

I watered your plants this morning.
I don't know any of their names,
Just that they're purple and red
And beautiful and need water,
And that you love them and that
Makes me love them too.
What I do know is 86 over 60,
Intercranial pressure, that the cerebellum
Should not slide into the spinal column.
Of course, I do know one of the plants.
The hanging pot is filled with strawberries.
The sun has baked them ripe as your lips.
They are warm, tender to the tongue.
      Delicious, needing water.

Saudade II

I started wearing your perfume
Last week after I ran out of
Aftershave, you know, your bottle
With the fancy flower shaped
Glass lid, I don't know the name,
And then I began wearing your pajamas,
The blue ones with the holes I should
Have replaced months ago. And I
Hope you're laughing as you
Read this, because of all my jobs—
Run to the grocery store at midnight
For mango ice cream guy,
I hate to say this because we're
Already in bed but I left my
Cellphone in the car guy, or honey,
The dog shit on the carpet guy—
My favorite job, the one I feel
I'm best at and enjoy most,
Is being your clown. I wasn't
Born a crusted set of pennies
Under the passenger side floor mat,
You just found me that way, camped
In a mattress in the living room,
Two crates for a dining room table,
A blender, plenty of dog food, the
Frig empty except a twelve of IPA,
So what I mean, what I'm trying
To say in some small way, is *Lady,*
Come home, soon, please come home.

Spoon Girl

The self we wish
Is not a self you've
Ever been or could be,
And that's okay. So
Think of a cloud sprinkled
With spring, cucumber
And lavender, the voice
Of our grandson
Humming a song
Brimming butterflies and
Raspberry candy,
Lighter than that cloud
As he tosses a ball
For our dog, his notes
Hibiscus sweet on
The ear's tongue.
Take this morning's spoon
You've been gifted
And ladle it dripping
With jam and laughter,
Stir in the plum of your lips
And a cardinal arcing
Across a dandelion field.
This hurts me:
You will never not hurt.
No dream can lift that
From the beautiful groove
Along your collarbone
Or reshape the cup
Of your skull to cease
The cerebellum's descent.
The pain must be,
The fox squirrel or
Rat snake that pirates
The robin's egg, deer fly

At the screen door,
Hare in the carrot patch.
I spoon you into midnight,
Root to valley, arm
Draping the moon
Of your hip, hyacinth
Nape timeless drunk adrift.
We will still dream,
Scoop deep in the sky,
Taste whatever fruit is sweet
And heavy on our vine.

What We Talk About When
We Talk About Love

Too many ways of looking
At a blackbird tossed
In the autumn sky.
From the dry shadows
Of the bed from which
The sun cannot step,
Your whisper flits above:
I am free to leave.
First, a living will,
Power of attorney,
No machines or tubes,
We first discussed this
When our hearts beat quick
In the raven's glimmer,
A clatter of wings burst
At red clay and live oak—
        Free to go.
The wind knows all directions.
I wipe feces from crevices
My tongue once explored,
I scrape uneaten meals
From cracked plates,
I dig arms under whatever
Is left to dig under—
So many ways of looking
At a blackbird thrown
In an autumn sky, life alit
In the few uncollapsed rivers
Of your hands, and I consider
The offer, freedom, mine from
You or yours from me not clear.
Stand with me, survey the distance:
Blanched earth, seedless,
Scab stubble frozen pools,

Creek frozen in its sheets,
The only proof of life its absence:
The bank gives way beneath our feet,
I grip the crest of your waist,
And one wing between us,
  We take flight.

Pre-Op

The hairnet is cute,
adorable French painter,
Lucille Ball chef,
a shoulder exposed
flowing electrode wires.
"We got this," she whispers,
but her eyes moisten.
The gurney wheels
unlock in an anvil jolt.
Her mouth forms the words
"I'm afraid" but I am quick
with a "We got this," knowing
all I've really got is the sliver
thinness of her hand
squeezed in mine.

I'm led back out
to the waiting pen.
It is nearly full but
no one is there.
Two chairs set face
to face form a bed.
I take my wife's jacket
from the plastic stow bag
and form a pillow.
I stuff the pillow beneath
my head, a sleeve hanging
loose, which I drape in
a bandage over my eyes.

Love With a Dying Woman

The night we met our tongues
jigged an insatiable fingertip tango—
we lapped ourselves full of our
deepest selves, a joyfest of fever and
delta wetland at the willing mouth
                    of a great river.

Now, desire an abandoned
house on a dark treeless street.
Roof shorn, doors and windows
kicked in, burned beams exposed.
Blood heat turned guilt-fire letter,
feeble inquiry, do you think
you're well enough tonight?
Pleasure trek off-ramped with pain—
                    to do, to do, *to do*?

I see your face across the park.
Glinting lips, toothy smile,
eyes warm as turned spring earth:
how lovely you truly are.
In the invalid gurney we've set up
in our living room, stairs to the king
sleigh bed overgrown in burr
and thistle, I brush your cheek.
Doe softness, but you cannot wake,
Tunneled deep into sleep.
I burrow into your side to wait out
the storm of the flesh's misery.
Holding you for what is always
perhaps the last time, I am sure,
somewhere, you do the same.

Everybody Gets It But You

Speak to speak in time,
note left on the kitchen table,
fading names scrawled on
cracked backs of photos, pyramid
drown in the drift of dunes, tags
sandblasted by another hail of echoes.
Leaf bud in the new spring wind:
the whistle of our movement,
trace of the lost jawline,
wanting to know something of
what strangeness we believed.
In our shadow, the pace petty,
a cairn of unmatched shoes, coats
only a fool would have worn,
armless statues, pocked columns,
bits, bytes, footprints, strewn
stones of someone's religion,
sepulchral pocket emptied of
lived lint and unlived hours.
I speak to myself. Admission:
the city was rigged against me,
dimed and nickeled in cheap wine,
no one's fault but the jackal—
I thought my way onto a highway
with no off-ramp circling
a mythical star, reciting todays
in a temple for tomorrows.

New morning post-op I come
to life alone at first light,
wash the sickness of dust
and charred crust of fear
from the sidewalk, root
deep against a dark sky
of expanding clouds.

I think of salutations...
We have this tomorrow.
I find your towel
from yesterday on
the edge of the bed,
still damp with your scent,
my every flesh drinking

Wonder Woman

Her favorite sleeping mask is adorned in leopard print. Jungle huntress. Sleek, powerful, unconquerable. Morning sunlight causes her headpain to spike and, medical bills still mounting, we can't afford blackout shades. While restful sleep is near impossible, she enjoys the stylish company of leopards. I am sitting across from the gurney we have set up in our bedroom next to the bed we used to share. She asks me if I've seen the eye mask. I find it on the floor between the beds.

"Here you go."

Her pain meds begin to kick in. Fentanyl, dilaudid, diazepam, whatever Hospice can provide. Her eyelids grow drunken, heavy. Her speech slurs, exacerbated by the neckbrace she must wear, which restricts movement of her jaw. The fifth— and we know final—brain surgery has shown no positive results. She places the eye mask on.

"I need my mask. Gonna be flying around."

"Oh yeah?"

"Yeah. Wonder Woman needs a mask."

"So where you flying to?"

"Everywhere. Gonna get the bad guys. Fly up over top them, swoop down. Kick ass and take names."

I take her hand. Thin. Pale. A papery whisp of light. She is a wonder. My wonder woman. My leopard queen. No primetime family friendly network time slot. No magic bracelets. No shield. No invisible plane, but she is taking flight, soaring off somewhere, eyes set on the infinite beyond. I am here on Earth, sitting on the bed we shared next to the gurney we brought in to give her some comfort, and I watch her drift off away from me to sleep.

What can I say about her?

I want her here.

What would I say *to* her, if she were awake, not taking to the clouds, soaring over everything, prowling through the high grass, fighting monsters and the malignant powers that forced her onto this gurney?

I cover her hand in both of mine.
I listen to her breathe.
Woman, I want you here.
I want you here.
I want you here.

More Praise for *A Temple for Tomorrows*:

"*A Temple for Tomorrows* is easily Jeffire's most important work. It is the gritty, steely and raw soul of a rooted Detroit native. From his opening poem "Birth Certificate" where he literally bursts into the world with all the rage of a Joe Louis fist, to his closing poem "Wonder Woman" where he loves and grieves resolutely like only a Motor City man can—Jeffire creates a roaring opus of words. This work moves like only a Detroit tale can. It's richly filled with stories of the complicated relationships we have with ourselves, family, lovers, and sprinkled with politics and revolutionary musings. *A Temple for Tomorrows* is just as emotionally opened as it is guarded—which is the highlight of its flawless brilliance. I found myself standing Penobscot straight with pride to be exposed to this masterpiece and to call its maestro my brother and friend.

—LaShaun phoenix Moore, author of *The Absence of Smoke and Mirrors*

"The authenticity of John Jeffire's voice is awe-inspiring—a smart, made-in-Detroit voice that knows the streets, what they offer and what they take away. He writes, "When my bones were made of bone / I stood Penobscot straight / and made my declarations / to priest and beat cop with equal parts / kiss my ass and reverence." Jeffire looks you in the eye as he confronts issues from war and injustice to living with the fear of his ailing wife's death. Grab a Kleenex before reading his beautifully crafted love poems. From "Saudade II": "I started wearing your perfume / last week after I ran out of aftershave, / you know, your bottle/ with the fancy flower shaped glass lid, and then / I began wearing your pajamas." *A Temple for Tomorrows* is an important collection, grounded in today's realities. Beneath Jeffire's bare-fisted grit you'll find a rhythmic pulse, not just his own, but one that beats for city and country. You trust this voice and feel at once vulnerable and protected."

—Diane Shipley-DeCillis, author of *Strings Attached*

"John Jeffire's polished verse in *A Temple for Tomorrows* sings a razor-edged lullaby without melancholy or sentimentality for raw-knuckled survivors. Written with clear-eyed confidence and skill, these poems offer hard-earned insight into the human dilemma."

—Linda K. Sienkiewicz, poet and author of *In the Context of Love*

"In the first poem of this stunning collection, Detroit poet John Jeffire, speaking of the day of his own birth, says, "I sprung dumb from the viaduct gutter.../ Backed up with rainbows of transmission fluid." These lines by Jeffire shovel coal, they kiss, they prostitute. They are a fifth of Black Label saved for a special occasion. These lines are rap, they are blues, they are tribute. Seriously, I've read nothing as honest as these poems. They come from a poet deeply in love with the mess that is this life, and the woman that is his wife. If all writing is guided by love, these poems are revolutionary; they riot against ignorance and protest on behalf of truth. They are earthquakes whose first rumbles are desire... Jeffire's poems are painted in the guts, gore, and tender images of everyday life. Yet they remind us that there are "Saints on strike in / A discarded century." The work here is both the siren and the silence after. It is Rock & Roll and the ringing buzz we carry home. I don't want to leave the concert of these poems."

—Joy Gaines-Friedler, author of *Capture Theory*

"John Jeffire's poems are challengingly and delightfully loaded with unrelenting voices and realities."

—Mark Wisniewski, author of *Watch Me Go*

"Hustler. Rough beast. Teacher. Right out of the gate John Jeffire's book shrieks. This puzzle is an homage of blood, family, war—shake downs, masques of shame, rotary phones, doing time. Its pieces are innumerable—chaos, surrender, soul, both penniless and proud; they are abandoned motels, saving face, steel and bone. They whisper Johnny Ace and a Wonder Woman. Detroit, America—eat your heart out. *A Temple for Tomorrows* kicks ass, takes names. At its core is an inimitable heart."

—Jim Reese, author of *Bone Chalk*

~

About the Author

John Jeffire was born in Detroit. In 2005, his novel *Motown Burning* was named Grand Prize Winner in the Mount Arrowsmith Novel Competition and in 2007 it won a Gold Medal for Regional Fiction in the Independent Publishing Awards. Jeffire's first book of poetry, *Stone + Fist + Brick + Bone,* was nominated for a Michigan Notable Book Award in 2009. Former U.S. Poet Laureate Philip Levine called the book "a terrific one for our city."

CPSIA information can be obtained
at www.ICGtesting.com
Printed in the USA
BVHW030006260721
612479BV00002B/152